空山不見人，但聞人語響。返
景入深林，復照青苔上。獨
坐幽篁裏，彈琴復長
嘯。深林人不知，明月
來相照 輞川集二首

POEMS OF SOLITUDE

寂寥集

POEMS OF SOLITUDE

TRANSLATED FROM THE CHINESE BY

JEROME CH'ÊN AND MICHAEL BULLOCK

CHARLES E. TUTTLE: PUBLISHERS
RUTLAND, VERMONT AND TOKYO, JAPAN

UNESCO COLLECTION OF REPRESENTATIVE WORKS

CHINESE SERIES

This book has been accepted in the
Chinese Literature Translations Series of the United Nations
Educational, Scientific and Cultural Organization
[UNESCO]

Published by the Charles E. Tuttle Co., Inc.
of Rutland, Vermont and Tokyo, Japan
with editorial offices at
Suido 1-chome, 2–6, Bunkyo-ku, Tokyo, Japan
by special arrangement with
Lund Humphries Publishers Ltd., London

The Morphological Development of Chinese Poetry 1

THE MORPHOLOGICAL DEVELOPMENT
OF CHINESE POETRY

The six poets represented in the following pages cover the mediaeval period, say roughly from the beginning of the Three Kingdoms [AD220] to that of the Sung [AD960]. Some important poets of the period, such as T'ao Ch'ien, Li Po and Tu Fu have been omitted either because their work has already been translated elsewhere or because their poems, as is the case with some of Tu Fu's, are virtually untranslatable. For historically determined reasons, all six of the poets gathered here lived lives of withdrawal from worldly affairs and they share the common theme of solitude and solitary meditation and reverie. Technically, on the other hand, they represent various phases in the evolution of Chinese poetry.

Archaic Chinese poetry underwent a change during the Han dynasty through contacts with foreign peoples and the importation of foreign music. New music demanded new words, hence new verse. The five-character lines were developed and matured during this dynasty, reaching their full development with the establishment of the Three Kingdoms. Juan's *Poems of My Heart* are all written in five-character lines, but with an indefinite number of lines. The rhyme occurs at the end of each even-number line and may change after every four or six lines. This style is called the Five-Character Ancient Style. T'ao Ch'ien of the Chin dynasty was its great master.

Towards the end of the Time of Division [AD580] poets began to use seven-character lines. A poem of this kind also has an indefinite number of lines; the rhyme

[1]

falls at the end of every even-number line and may change as the poem proceeds. This is known as the Seven-Character Ancient Style. Pao Chao's *Tedious Ways* are written in this form.

Also at the end of the Time of Division, scholars began to take an interest in phonetics. A promising start was made with the study of rhymes and tones, and the terms Even Tones and Oblique Tones were invented. Much thought was given to the theory and principles of poetics, with the result that a network of rules and regulations was woven and imposed on poetry. The so-called Modern Styles thus began. They had three distinct characteristics: 1. they were mostly short, in four or eight lines; 2. there was an emphasis on parallelism; and 3. on phonetics. They were the prelude to the poetry of the T'ang.

Although the Ancient Styles were still being used, the predominant styles of the T'ang poetry were:

Five-Character Four Line – rhyme occurs at the end of each even-number line, having been set in the first, and it is mostly even-tone rhyme. [*Poems of the River Wang*].

Five-Character Eight Line – rhyme also occurs at the end of each even-number line, in even tones, and the tone of every character used is *regulated*, either an even- or oblique-tone word. Therefore this is called the Five-Character Regulated Style. Another feature of this style is that the second couplet must be parallel word by word. When the second word in the first line is a numeral, for instance, the second word of the second line must be another numeral.

Seven-Character Four Line – same as the Five-Character Four Line.

Seven-Character Eight Line – same as the Five-Character Eight Line, called the Seven-Character Regulated Style.

All these styles are represented among the poems by Li Ho translated here.

[2]

In the T'ang dynasty, however, China's contact with the world at large widened. More new music was imported into China. New verse was again in demand. The even-length lines did not seem to meet it. At first, musicians added a few meaningless words to fit the tunes, thus breaking the golden rule of equal length. This was the beginning of the *tz'ŭ*.

Poets did not "write" *tz'ŭ* but "filled" them. The expression shows how strict are the rules of the *tz'ŭ*. The tone of each word is fixed, so is the tone of the rhyme. A *tz'ŭ* is normally divided into two stanzas. The same rhyme runs through a whole stanza, but a new rhyme may be used in the next. Li Yü was a great master of this style. Many titles of his *tz'ŭ* are almost incomprehensible, because they are the titles of foreign melodies transliterated into Chinese. The *tz'ŭ* began at the end of the T'ang, developed in the Five Dynasties [AD904–959] and was perfected during the Sung. After that, Chinese poetry lapsed into sterility, except for librettos for operas performed under the Mongol rule.

阮步兵詠懷詩

JUAN CHI

[210–263]

Fifteen Poems of My Heart

Juan Chi lived in the romantic period known as the Three Kingdoms [220–264] when the Wei controlled the north and the Wu and the Shu shared the south of China. The Wei was the largest of the three, ruled by the Ts'ao family. Juan Chi was a northerner, the son of a great scholar, Juan Yü, who was one of the Seven Men of Letters of the Chien-an reign [196–219].

In his adult life, Juan Chi witnessed the transfer of power from the Ts'ao to the Ssǔ-ma family, who first served the Ts'ao as ministers and commanders and eventually usurped the throne and unified China to found the Chin dynasty in 265. The long process of transfer was a painful one. Ssǔ-ma I rose to power during the reign and after the death of the first Emperor of the Wei, but he only gained control over the Army after the death of Marshal Ts'ao Chên in 251. His progress as a warlord was helped by the continual wars between the Wei and the Shu and, as might be expected, his path was spattered with blood. In 249, he staged a *coup d'état* which seriously crippled the authority of the Imperial clan. Many influential people, including the Commander-in-Chief of the Army, were killed. His sons, Ssǔ-ma Ssǔ and Ssǔ-ma Chao continued to weaken the Ts'ao family by crushing the uprisings against them led by Kuan Ch'iu-chien and Chu-kê Tan, as well as by putting many important ministers to death. It was a period when the life of every famous man was in constant danger.

The Juan family, like many other educated people of that time, were loyal to the Wei. None of them had any political or military power of his own. Their moral convictions would not allow them to ally themselves with a family which was about to usurp the throne;

[9]

B

nevertheless, they fully realized the grave danger of struggling against it. Furthermore, the usurpation was clearly to be cunningly dressed up in the cloak of a hundred virtues. Under such circumstances, men of fame had to have sufficiently convincing excuses for staying out of politics. Very few of them succeeded, but Juan Chi was one of them.

His "escapism" was evolved on two levels. He and his friends, notably Hsi K'ang, developed a political philosophy which was akin to both Taoism and Anarchism. They attacked the government, the ruling class, the moral code and the law. As serious philosophical thought, it was coherent and persuasive; and as an escapist's apology it was honourable. On the second level, Juan Chi and his friends affected an eccentricity which became the fashion of the period. He and six other eminent scholars often met in a bamboo grove where they drank, always excessively, composed poems, discussed philosophy and played the lute. They were known as the Seven Sages of the Bamboo Grove.

A few anecdotes will suffice to describe their idiosyncracies.

Ssŭ-ma Chao, the Prince of Chin, wanted his son [later the founder Emperor of the Chin] to marry Juan Chi's daughter. He approached Juan, but only to find him continuously drunk for sixty days. The project was eventually dropped.

A young man, Chung Hui, who was obviously a spy of the Ssŭ-ma family, wanted to discuss politics with Juan, but he never found him sober.

Juan Chi asked to be the Chief of the Infantry Kitchen, because it had an excellent cellar.

Juan Chi received people by showing either the

pupils of his eyes or only the whites. The pupils were reserved for his friends, while ceremonial, and therefore vulgar, visitors were deprived of the privilege.

Juan Chi often drove a chariot alone and, as a rule, he lost the way and wept bitterly.

A prefect went to see him. They stayed together for a whole day during which Juan did not utter a single word.

Such a man was obviously not fit for responsibility.

Philosophy and eccentricity alone might not have been enough to save his neck. His close friend, Hsi K'ang, for instance, shared his philosophy and behaved in an even stranger manner. Yet he was executed, for he had a bad temper. Juan Chi, on the other hand, managed to show neither his anger nor his joy.

It is in his poems that we see his true self. He left among other literary works eighty-two *Poems of My Heart* of which fifteen are translated here.

POEMS OF MY HEART

[1]

Being sleepless at midnight,
I rise to play the lute.
The moon is visible through the curtains
And a gentle breeze sways the cord of my robe.
A lonely wild-goose cries in the wilderness
And is echoed by a bird in the woods.
As it circles, it gazes
At me, alone, imbued with sadness.

[2]

In my youth,
I too was fond of singing and dancing.
I went west to the Capital
And frequented the Li's and the Chao's.
Before the fun came to an end,
I realized time had been wasted.
On my return journey,
I looked back at the riverside district
Where I had squandered a great deal,
So that not a coin was left.
Coming to the T'ai-hang mountain path,
I was afraid of again losing my way.

[3]
The last rays of the setting sun,
Which once shone upon me warmly, have
        now gone.
The wind keeps returning to strike the walls
While cold birds seek warmth in one another's
        breast.
Clinging to their feathers,
They fear hunger in silence.
O, men of influence
Remember to withdraw in time!
You look sad and frail.
Is it because of power and fame?
I prefer to fly with jays and tits,
Not with hoary herons.
For they travel high and far,
Making the return too hard.

[4]

Weird dances are performed in the north
        street
And near the river decadent songs are heard.
These flighty, leisured youths,
Enslaved by fads and fashions,
Always take a short cut
To sensual pleasure.
I see no one racing against the sun
Or turning his staff into a forest.
The recipe for a long life
Alone calms my heart.

[5]

Autumn is beginning, the weather is turning
       chill.
Crickets move in to sing under my bed.
A thousand things surge into my mind
And grieve my heart.
A thousand tales search for words;
But to whom will they be told?
The morning breeze flows under my sleeves,
The moonlight thins,
And the cock crows,
As I turn my horses' heads towards home.

[6]

Sitting in an empty hall
I enjoy no one's company.
Going out to the endless road
I see no chariot or horse.
Climbing up a hill
I look at places far away.
A solitary bird hovers
And a stray beast wanders.
The setting sun reminds me of relatives and
       friends.
How I have longed to talk to them!

[7]
Inscribe on your heart
Every inch of the time at sunset.
Adjust your sleeves, unsheathe a slender sword,
And look up at the passing clouds.
Among them a dark stork
Raises its head and rattles its beak.
Darting aloft, it vanishes into the sky.
Never again will it be heard.
It is no company for the cuckoos and the crows
That circle round the Court.

[8]
Day and night
Revolve,
While my face wrinkles
And my spirit wanes,
But the sight of injustice still pains me.
One change induces another
That cannot be dealt with by tact or wit.
The cycle goes on for ever.
I only fear that in a moment
Life will disperse in the wind.
I have always trodden on thin ice.
Yet no one knows!

[9]
Morning and evening
Alternate,
While my complexion ages
And my strength ebbs.
Wine only arouses sadness
And reminds me of friends and bygone days.
What have I to relate
Except untold sorrow and regret?
My wish is to plough the fields,
Yet who is there to share my hermitage?
Bitterness and virtuous deeds
Have done me much damage.
Why do I curl up and hibernate?
To hide underground among serpents and dragons.

[10]
His influence —
        the scorching sun or a torrential river —
Extends a myriad miles.
His bow hangs in the tree
        on which the sun rests.
His sword leans
        against the place where the sky ends.
Mountains are his whetstones;
And the Yellow River is long enough to be his belt.
But in the eyes of a wise recluse,
Size is of the least importance.
For a giant corpse
Only feeds more vultures.
Perhaps it is only for this
That heroes and aspirants achieve fame and merit.

[11]
I do not see my star in the sky
But tear-drops on my sleeves.
Courtly birds fly high;
Only sparrows dwell in lowly bushes.
As I play the lute and sigh,
A black cloud hangs over my house.
On lofty cliffs cranes cry,
But their example is not for me to follow.

[12]
As dew-drops freeze,
Green grass wilts.
Gentlemen do not understand this,
Yet are said to be wise.
Let me ride on a cloud
To visit the immortals.

[13]
I will not learn to ride a winged horse,
Fearing it will leave me to weep at a lonely
      roadside.
I dive low or fly high
To avoid the trap of a net.
I float a light boat
And gaze into the boundless waves.
It is better to forget in a river or a lake
Than to wet one another with bubbles on
      stony dry land.
Seldom can I be arrayed to look elegant,
My way is to be sincere and prudent.
The ancient immortals
Will help me
To survive this long and fearful night.

[14]
Once I dressed up
To receive a guest
Who was strange to me
And airy like a grain of flying dust.
Clouds trailed after his robes.
His subtle words were pearls,
So short a time did he remain.
When shall I meet him again?

[15]
I am growing old
In the shadow of death.
My admiration goes to the waves
That come from the same source
            to flow in different ways.
Life is not worthy of mention
Yet hate and enmity have been my tribulation.
Do I really have adversaries?
Or are my sensitive ears deceiving my eyes?
Vision and hearing are both waning.
But malice against me is still waxing.
I shall call on my Taoist friends;
Together we shall go on a journey.

鮑明遠

舞鶴賦

行路難

PAO CHAO
[414-466]

Eighteen Tedious Ways

The Ruined City

C

The tottering Empire of Chin [265–420] came and went. Much of its downfall should be attributed to the invasions of the Huns, Tartars, Tibetans and other tribal peoples, to the strife among the princes, and to the corruption of the ruling class. With the founding of the Liu Sung dynasty [420–479], the division of China became clear. The north was ruled by the Tartar dynasty of Wei, leaving the south to the Liu family. The tense relations between these two empires were punctuated by numerous frontier skirmishes and occasional full-scale wars. The strengthening of the defences was a necessity and a heavy burden on the more peace-loving south. This major division persisted until the reunification by the Sui and the T'ang.

Pao Chao was doubly fortunate in having lived during the long and prosperous reign of the Yüan-chia [424–453] over the southern empire, and in having achieved great literary fame and high office at a time when class distinctions were perhaps at their most intense, in spite of being the son of a peasant. He served first in Prince Lin-ch'uan's secretariat and then in those of the Princes Hêng-yang and Shih-hsing. The last-named rebelled in 453 at the end of the Yüan-chia reign, and Pao Chao met his first setback after the rebellion was suppressed. Three years later, he was rehabilitated and appointed prefect of Yung-chia. In 459, he paid a visit to the devastated city of Kuang-ling, the result of which was his poem *The Ruined City*. Another three years later, when he was forty-eight, Pao Chao joined Prince Lin-hai's secretariat and toured West China with his master. In 466, this Prince also staged a rebellion against the throne.

The revolt was fruitless and Pao was killed in the defeat.

The Yüan-chia was a famous reign in the history of Chinese literature. But Pao Chao was in a sense a lone wolf, for his style, straightforward and unconstrained, was in sharp contrast to the prevalent floweriness of Yên Yên-chih, Hsieh Ling-yün and so on. His *Tedious Ways* are believed to have been written when he was twenty. This, however, is only supported by flimsy evidence. A more acceptable supposition is that they were composed over a long period of time, since they refer to various stages of Pao's life.

TEDIOUS WAYS

[1]
To you, my master,
    vintage wine in a gold cup,
    a carved lute in a jade box,
    a silk net of hibiscus pink,
    and a satin bed-cover embroidered with grapes.
My rosy cheeks are fading away
Like the year, or the dimming light of the day.
Pray, master, cease grieving and meditating,
And listen to my Song of the Tedious Ways.
Do you not see the decaying Platforms
    of the Cypress Beam and the Bronze Bird?
Would you not prefer the serene music of bygone
    days?

[2]
This burner comes from a famous master of Loyang
    – purified, hammered and fired
      and then engraved with the beauty of Ch'in
        holding her lover's hand.
For you and the pleasure of tonight,
It is now placed in the bright candlelight
    and inside the net canopy.
On its outer surface shine the scales of a dragon,
And the purple scent of muskdeer streams out from
    within.
If one day your heart changes,
I shall gaze at it and weep for a hundred years.

[3]

Up above the marble steps, in the perfumed chambers,
Behind the painted screens,
Golden Orchid lives.
Her attire is the softest of silk
And her work is to pick vanilla flowers.
Swallows dart hither and thither
As the wind shakes down plum blossom.
She draws back the curtains,
      raises a lonely cup of wine,
With a song in her throat and tears in her eyes.
How often does life bring happiness?
Would she not prefer to be one of those geese
      in pairs in the wilderness,
Or the solitary crane in the clouds?

[4]

When you throw water on the floor,
It runs in all directions.
Life has its predestinations.
Then it is useless
      to worry about everything.
Before you sing the Tedious Ways,
Comfort yourself and pour some wine.
I am not made of stone or wood.
For lack of courage,
      I prefer to remain silent.

[5]
Do you not see, my love,
    the grass on the river bank
Withers in the winter
    only to grow again in the spring?
Do you not see, my love,
    the sun above the city wall
Sinks tonight
    only to rise again tomorrow morning?
But we are different –
Once gone, we never return.
Life is rarely pleasant.
Try to enjoy here and now.
I wish my visits could be more frequent
And that I always had money for wine.
I have no time for fame or wealth.
Heaven takes care of my life and death.

[6]
Food on the table
Does not induce me to eat.
I unsheathe my sword,
    strike at the pillar
      and lament.
How long must I hop
    with my wings folded?
So I resign my post;
Go home for a rest.
At dawn, I bid farewell to my parents;
At dusk, I return to them again.
My children play with me in the bedroom
While I watch my wife weaving with the loom.

Since ancient times, saints and sages
  have always been poor and modest.
Their way of life is what I now choose.

[7]
Riding through the northern gate
Sorrow suddenly seizes me.
On looking around, I can only see
Pines and cypresses growing on desolate tombs.
In their blue gloom
A nightjar perches.
It is said to be the spirit of an ancient king.
Its dirge never ceases
And its dishevelled feathers
Bristle like the hair of a convict.
It flies from branch to branch
Searching for worms and ants.
Has it forgotten its majesty?
Many changes are not to be expected.
My heart, overladen with grief,
  knows no answer.

[8]
Five peach trees grow in my garden.
One of them has begun to bloom.
It is now the charming third moon
And the wind blows the petals
  to a neighbour's home
Where the lonely mistress weeps
With a hand on her bosom and her lapel wet.
When her husband left,
There was no thought of a long parting.

Yet now dust covers the couch
    and the mirror no longer reflects.
Her robes are growing loose, her hair untidy.
Can she be happy again?
    Can she stop pacing to and fro till midnight?

[9]
Cut the silk and dye it yellow;
But it is too tangled to be unravelled.
When we first met,
You thought we suited each other.
We took the oath:
Through thick and thin, life and death,
We should never separate.
Now my beauty has gone
And there is nothing to hold your interest.
Here, I return your gold pin and turtle-shell clips.
I do not want to keep them,
    for fear of melancholy memories.

[10]
Do you not see, my master, the hibiscus?
Its beauty seldom lasts a day.
The young in their gaudy splendour
Will soon follow the same path,
From which there is no return.
For a thousand autumns
Nothing will be heard of them.
Their lonely spirits will walk to and fro
    on empty paths or round their tombs.
They will perhaps hear birds chanting in the wind,
But be quite unable to recall bygone days.

[33]

Let us be each other's comfort
And think of them no more.

[11]
Do you not see the fallen leaves
        that rustle on the pavings and steps;
Will they become green again?
Do you not see the sacrificial food and wine
        that are laid out for the spirits,
Who have never once raised the cups?
To you, this should be a loud warning
That life passes like lightning;
Youthful days never return;
And there cannot be time to compete against anyone.
Retain your noble aims;
Enjoy your food and friends.
For they alone can repel
Your worries and fear.
Yet you still look unhappy.
Do you not like my Tedious Ways?

[12]
In the last spring, flowers smothered the orchard;
In the next winter, snow will cover the hill-tops.
O, seasons come and go.
But from you, at the lonely frontiers, not a word.
It has been three autumns
Since I last held your sleeves
        and bade you farewell.
The morning grief has crystallized into tears
And the evening sorrow woven into a web round my
        heart.

I have not touched rouge or perfume
                    for many moons;
Nor set a pin in my tousled hair.
Dust flies from the curtains and screens
To settle on the disused powder jars and vanity box.
Is life an eternal woe?
Or is it the woe that keeps one alive?

[13]
The cheeping of spring chicks on the steps
Takes my thoughts back home.
When I first came with high hopes,
I enjoyed the army life.
Three years drifted away.
The other day, I was alarmed
        by my hair going grey.
In the evening, I pulled the white ones out
        near the river;
Only to find, next morning,
        that they had grown again.
After that I began to fear
        that I should die here as a wanderer;
That my regrets, being rootless,
        would transform me into a wandering ghost.
Every time I think of my home,
I also think of my people lamenting.
Suddenly a stranger comes to me
Saying that he knows my family.
"I have stayed in your town
And was told that you were in this place
        holding office.
I have travelled thousands of miles

[35]

On the way to a garrison post.
Before I set out, I heard that your good lady,
        lived like a widow,
            slept alone,
And had the reputation of being chaste.
I also heard that her eyes
            were never free from tears
And she herself withered and aged,
That she used no make-up,
That she looked pitiful.
This, I hope you will never forget.''

[14]
Do you not see the young men
Going to the frontiers?
        Probably they will never return.
Day and night
        they will long for a letter.
But the rivers and mountain passes
        will always dash their hopes.
The desert wind chases away scraps of white cloud
And barbarian strings accuse and embitter the cold.
Their saddening notes spiral up the hills
        to look south.
O, the youthful faces,
        have they changed?
Will barbarian horses trample them to death?
Will they escape to be reunited with their families?
Life is unending tedium
        about which I have nothing else to say,
But to stand up and draw a deep breath.

[15]

Do you not see the Platform of the Cypress Beam?
Now it is only rubble and weeds.
Do you not see the old palaces
Taken over by quails and mists?
Where are the singers and dancers?
On the slopes there lie so many graves.
Their long sleeves were once deadly rivals
When worn by precious mistresses.
Did they drink and make merry when they were
     alive?
Now, underground, do they grieve?

[16]

Do you not see the frost setting on the ice?
It stiffens the chill
And will not soften
In the morning sunshine.
Let life take its own course.
It is idle to force it.
As time goes on,
My hair grows thinner and greyer,
     quite unable to bear my hat any longer.

[17]

Do you not see the birds in the spring?
When they first came,
     hundreds of flowers bloomed.
But now the chilly wind
Makes them fade all the faster.
Time relentlessly passes
As my sorrow deepens.

[18]

It is no use grumbling over being poor.
Fortune is beyond one's control.
Do your best at forty.
If you are only twenty,
    there is a great deal for you to know.
Do not abandon yourself to the snow,
For times will change, spring will come
    and luck will turn.
Be happy and sing your Tedious Ways.
For my part I only wish
    that my bottles may be full;
And that under my pillows,
    there may always be money to buy some more.
For a single year's joy is far better
    than a century's labour and toil.

THE RUINED CITY

The immense plain
   runs south to the foamy waves of the sea
   and north to the purple passes of the Great Wall.
In it
   canals are cut through the valleys;
And rivers and roads
   lead to every corner.

In its golden past,
   axles of chariots and carts
   often rubbed against each other
   like men's shoulders.
Shops and houses stood row upon row
And laughter and songs rose up from them.
Glittering and white were the salt fields;
Gloomy and blue were the copper mines.
Wealth and talents
And cavalry and infantry
Reinforced the strict and elaborate
Regulations and laws.
Winding moats and lofty walls
Were dug and built, to ensure
That prosperity would long endure.
People were busy working
On palaces and battlements
And ships and beacon stations
Up and down, far and wide
At all places.
Magnets[1] were installed at mountain passes;
Red lacquer was applied to doors and gates.

[1] To attract enemy arrows

[39]

The strongholds and fortresses
   would see to it
That for a myriad generations
   the family's rule should last.
But after five centuries or three dynasties
The land was divided like a melon,
Or shared like beans.

Duckweed flourishes in the wells
And brambles block the roads.
Skunks and snakes dwell on sacred altars
While muskdeer and squirrels quarrel on marble steps.
In rain and wind,
Wood elves, mountain ghosts,
Wild rats and foxes
   yawp and scream from dusk to dawn.
Hungry hawks grind their beaks
As cold owls frighten the chicks in their nests.
Tigers and leopards hide and wait
   for a drink of blood
   and a feast of flesh.
Fallen tree-trunks lie lifelessly across
Those once busy highways.
Aspens have long ceased to rustle
And grass dies yellow
In this harsh frosty air
Which grows into a cruelly cold wind.
A solitary reed shakes and twists,
And grains of sand, like startled birds,
   are looking for a safe place to settle.
Bushes and creepers, confused and tangled,
   seem to know no boundaries.

[41]

D

They pull down walls
And fill up moats.
And beyond a thousand miles
Only brown dust flies.
Deep in my thoughts, I sit down and listen
To this awesome silence.

Behind the painted doors and embroidered curtains
There used to be music and dancing.
Hunting or fishing parties were held
In the emerald forests or beside the marble pools.
The melodies from various states
And works of art and rare fish and horses
Are all now dead and buried.
The young girls from east and south
Smooth as silk, fragrant as orchids,
White as jade with their lips red,
Now lie beneath the dreary stones and barren earth.

The greatest displeasure of the largest number
Is the law of nature.
For this ruined city,
I play the lute and sing:
"As the north wind hurries on,
    the battlements freeze.
They tower over the plain
    where there are neither roads nor field-paths.
For a thousand years and a myriad generations,
    I shall watch you to the end in silence."

王摩诘

裴十廸

辋川集

WANG WEI
[699-759]

P'EI TI
[714 - ?]

Forty Poems of the River Wang

The seventy-six years from 684 to 760, the golden period of the T'ang dynasty, form one of the most interesting chapters in the history of China.

In 684, the able but notorious Empress Wu seized the throne by unsavoury means, and during her reign the empire underwent significant changes. The traditional policy of keeping the seat of the administrative authority in the Kuan-chung [the present-day Shensi province], which had been pursued since the founding of the dynasty in 618, was gradually abandoned. Although the Kuan-chung and the south-east provinces were still directly controlled by the central government, the rest of the empire was divided into military districts and placed under local commanders who were mostly Sinicized tribal leaders.

Meanwhile the reins of the central government slowly slipped out of the fingers of the Imperial clan and the noble families of the Kuan-chung. In their stead, a new ruling class arose, chiefly men of letters of pure Chinese origin, selected for high offices through open competitive examinations. *Chin-shih*, the highest degree awarded to successful candidates, replaced letters of recommendation as the avenue to distinction.

Relations between the Chinese literati and non-Chinese military governors were not always as harmonious as the rulers of a unified empire would have liked to see. Friction between them opened the door to another influential clique, viz., the court eunuchs from the south-west. They were not Han-Chinese and their rapid rise to power increased the political complexities of the period.

By the middle of the eighth century, the authority of the Imperial family had become quite nominal.

Under these circumstances, ambitious men of the military class felt themselves sufficiently powerful to challenge the government for the Heavenly Mandate. One such challenge was the An Lu-shan Rebellion, which broke out in 755, brought devastation to the northern provinces, and was not suppressed until three years later. Then began the decline of the dynasty.

*

The unity of the empire became increasingly dependent upon cultural ties. This may explain the intense activity in philosophy and the arts, productive of great achievements, during this period. The government's attitude towards such activities was in general liberal, and cultural contacts with foreign countries were frequent. Early in the seventh century, Hsüan-chuang went to India and brought back at the end of his seventeen years' visit a large number of Buddhist *sutras*. He devoted his last years to their translation into Chinese and it was owing to him, and to a lesser extent to other leading monks and preachers, that Buddhism gained its tremendous popularity in China. The Empress Wu herself was an ardent follower and patron of the new religion. Her grandson, the Emperor Hsüan-tsung [reigned from 712 to 755], though a Taoist, was never too harsh in his treatment of the Buddhists. The Court's religious tolerance even extended to Nestorianism and Manichaeism, whose temples were to be found in the Imperial Capital.

The government also encouraged literary and artistic studies. Landscape painting became well developed in this period and Wang Wei himself excelled in it. Never before or after, in her long history, did China produce so many accomplished poets and calligraphers in so short a period. The writing of short stories began to flourish and a new music to emerge. "It was regarded as a disgrace," as the historian records, "if a boy in his teens could not discuss literature with his guests." It was in this political and cultural background that our poets, Wang Wei and P'ei Ti, were born.

*

Wang Wei has always ranked much higher as a poet than his neighbour in Wang-ch'uan, P'ei Ti, not only today but even among his contemporaries. He was born in 699 as the son of a minor official of T'ai-yüan in Shansi. Two years later another great poet, Li Po, was born; but these two famous men of letters were very different in temperament and were to have little contact with each other throughout their lives.

Wang Wei was the eldest of five brothers, of whom only he and his second brother, Chin, achieved a literary reputation. His prose attracted the attention of discriminating minds when he was only nine, and many of his poems written at the age of fifteen are preserved and still read.

A gifted young man like Wang Wei was obviously destined for the *Chin-shih* examination and an official career. The degree was much coveted and the competition extremely keen – normally a hundred or so were chosen from a field of two or three thousand. Wang

[49]

Wei set out for the capital for this purpose when he was nineteen. With his poems and music, he impressed and won the esteem of Prince Ch'i. By the Prince, he was presented at the Court of the eldest Princess, where he recited his odes and played the *p'i-pa* with great skill. His good looks and artistry pleased the Imperial lady, who promised to do whatever she could to bring about his success in the next *Chin-shih* examination. At the age of twenty, Wang Wei was honoured with the learned title of *Chin-shih* of the Empire.

His career as an official, however, did not run nearly so smoothly. He was first appointed court musician, a post from which he was soon degraded, being put in charge of the granary of Chi-chou. This setback was reversed when Chang Chiu-ling was made the Grand Secretary to the Court, for Chang was one of the literary dignitaries of the time; Wang Wei was promoted by him first to a secretaryship in the Grant Secretariat, then to a censorship in the Palace Censorate, and finally to the post of senior clerk of the State Treasury. This progress came to an abrupt halt when Wang Wei's mother died. .

Grief over his mother's death nearly killed him. After the mourning period, he resumed his official career as a senior clerk in the Board of Civil Office and was soon transferred to the post of Court Secretary. It was then, in 755 when he was fifty-six, that the Great Rebellion broke out which drove the Emperor, Hsüan-tsung, into exile.

At this time Wang Wei was an invalid, suffering from dysentry, and thus unable to follow the hurried Imperial Progress to Szechuan. The capital was

overrun by the rebels and their leader, An Lu-shan,
"invited" Wang Wei to Lo-yang – the rebels' capital.
His poems in captivity revealed his loyalty to the
T'ang and were to save him from punishment when
the Rebellion was suppressed. His brother, Chin, the
Vice-President of the Board of Punishment in the
Court of the new Emperor, Hsü-tsung, begged his
master to deprive him of office and rank instead of
penalizing Wang Wei.

Wang Wei was pardoned and received an appoint-
ment in the Palace of the Heir Apparent. Shortly
afterwards the Emperor restored him to the post of
Court Secretary and subsequently promoted him to
the exalted office of Vice-President of the Right. He
was then fifty-eight.

*

Wang Wei married young, but by this time he had
been a widower for thirty years. He never remarried.
The tragic loss of his mother and wife may have
prompted him to embrace Buddhism, a religion to
which his devotion grew stronger towards the end of
his life. He became a vegetarian, dressed very plainly
and went to live in his newly acquired country
retreat in Lan-t'ien.

Lan-t'ien was not far to the south of the capital,
and there two mountains met to form the Wang-
ch'uan Valley. A river rushed through the valley
northward to Pa – the River Wang. And along the
perpendicular cliffs on both sides were cut narrow
and dangerous footpaths, which allowed the entrance

[51]

of eager hermits but discouraged the less adventurous common people. Behind this difficult pass the land flattened out in a rectangular stretch about seven miles in length. Here Sung Chih-wên, a poet of the Empress Wu's reign, had built his secluded residence, and the property now came into the possession of Wang Wei.

In this lonely studio of his there were little else but his tea service, drug crucibles, *sutra* desk, incense burner, pouffe and hammock. He had one or two boys to attend to the household duties. Here he meditated and studied the Buddhist classics. The studio was frequented by his friends. Together they played the lute and composed poems. Forty of these poems were included in his anthology, *Wang-ch'uan Chi* [Poems of the River Wang] of which twenty were written by himself and twenty by P'ei Ti.

We know pitifully little about P'ei, except that he was fifteen years younger than Wang Wei. Very few of his poems, apart from those in the *Wang-ch'uan Chi*, are preserved. He left Wang-ch'uan, probably upon appointment to some office, before Wang Wei's death. Wang wrote to him:

One night I climbed up the Hua-tzŭ hill, to watch the reflection of the moon in the River Wang. The mountains seemed unable to sustain the cold, and the lights beyond the woods in the distance blinked. Dogs barked wildly; they too felt the chill. There was also the sound of the washer-women's pounding, punctuated by the tolling of the bells. I returned to my studio and sat in silence with my page boys. I recalled the days when you were here and composed poems with me. Spring will come again. Flowers will bloom, fish come up for the sun, egrets and pheasants fly hither and thither and dew drops wet the grass. Could you join me once more?

He also sent P'ei a poem:

> Leaning upon my staff.
> I stand in front of the gate.
> The song of cicadas
> is brought to me by the evening wind.
> On the far side of the ferry
> the sun is setting
> And above the cottage
> a solitary curl of smoke is rising.

One day in the seventh month of 759, Wang Wei asked for a writing brush and paper and wrote several letters to his brother and friends. Then he died.

THE COVE OF THE WALL OF MÊNG

WANG: My new house
        is at the beginning of the wall of Mêng,
Among old trees
        and remains of decaying willows.
The other, after me,
        who will he be?
Vain his grief
        for this which was mine.

P'EI: *My new hut*
        is under the old wall:
Occasionally I go up
        to the ancient enclosure.
There is nothing of the past now
        about the old wall;
Men of today, uncaring,
        come and go.

THE HILL OF HUA-TZŬ

WANG: The birds fly away
      into infinite space:
Over the whole mountain
      returns the splendour of autumn.
Ascending and descending
      Hua-tzŭ hill,
I feel
      unbounded bewilderment and
        lamentation.

P'EI: *The sun sets,*
      the wind rises among the pines.
Returning home,
      there is a little dew upon the grass.
The reflection of the clouds
      falls into the tracks of my shoes,
The blue of the mountains
      touches my clothes.

THE HERMITAGE AMONG THE
MAIDENHAIR TREES

WANG: Maidenhair timber
        cut into beams,
Fragrant reeds
        interwoven for the planks,
Who knows
        if the clouds from the ceiling
Have gone to carry
        rain among men?

P'EI: *Far, far away*
        is the maidenhair hut;
I have ascended the hillside
        so many times already.
In the south the mountain-tops,
        in the north the lakes;
I see them in front of me,
        then I look back over my shoulder.

E

THE HILL OF THE
HATCHET-LEAVED BAMBOOS

WANG: The tall bamboos
        soar to the sky
        and their tops bend.
  The deep blue
        in the slight movement of the waves
        trembles.
  I walk along
        the unfamiliar Shang hill-roads
  Which even the woodman
        does not know.

P'EI: *In the white moonlight the stream*
        winds its way
        and disappears from sight.
  The green of the bamboos
        grows denser,
        and then spills over.
  Without pause
        I push on along the mountain road;
  I walk and sing,
        my eyes on the familiar summits.

THE DEER ENCLOSURE

WANG: On the lonely mountain
      I meet no one,
I hear only the echo
      of human voices.
At an angle the sun's rays
      enter the depths of the wood,
And shine
      upon the green moss.

P'EI: *At the end of the day*
      the mountain looks cold.
But a belated wanderer
      still passes on his way.
He knows nothing
      of the life of the wood:
Nothing remains
      but the tracks of the buck.

THE MAGNOLIA ENCLOSURE

WANG: The mountain receives
    the last rays of autumn:
Flocks of birds follow
    the first flights.
A flash of emerald
    flares out from time to time.
The darkness of evening
    has nowhere to rest.

P'EI: *From the vault of light*
    at the going down of the sun,
The voices of the birds
    mingle with the voice of the torrent.
The path beside the stream
    winds into the distance;
Joy of solitude,
    will you ever come to an end?

THE BAY OF HERB-OF-GRACE

WANG: When the fruit is maturing
        still red and green,
    It is as though the trees
        were once more in flower.
    To the guest who is staying
        among the mountains
    I offer
        this cup of hibiscus.

P'EI: *The mingled perfume of pepper plant and*
        cassia eddies by,
    The leaves drift
        among the tall bamboos.
    Even the setting sun
        shines through the clouds;
    In the bosky depths
        there lingers a sense of chill.

THE PATH OF THE ASHTREES

WANG: On the narrow path,
        sheltered by the ashtrees
In the secrecy of their shade
        flourishes the green moss,
Only swept
        when someone answers the gate,
Fearing that the monk from the mountain
        has come to call.

P'EI: *To the south of the gate,*
        along by the ashtrees,
Is the path over the hill-crest,
        that leads to Lake I.
When the autumn comes
        it rains much on the mountain;
No one picks up
        the falling leaves.

THE PAVILION OF THE LAKE

WANG: Light the boat that carries me
      to meet the gentle guest,
Who from a great distance
      is coming over the lake.
Then, on the terrace,
      before a cup of wine,
On every side
      the lotus flowers will open.

P'EI: *In front of the balcony,*
      as the expanse of water
      fills with ripples,
The solitary moon
      goes wandering without pause.
From the depth of the valley
      the cries of the monkeys rise;
Borne by the wind
      they reach me in my room.

NAN-CH'A

WANG: Gaily the boat
>> sails towards Nan-Ch'a,
> Pei-chai, on the waves,
>> is almost out of sight.
> Beyond the bay,
>> I discern men and houses,
> Far, far away.
>> I cannot identify them.

P'EI: *Alone, the boat*
>> *rests where the wind carries it.*
> *At Nan-Ch'a, the waters of the lake*
>> *beat against the rugged shore.*
> *The sun sinks,*
>> *goes down into the Yên-tzǔ.*
> *The limpid billows vanish*
>> *in the immense expanse.*

LAKE I

WANG: The voice of the flute
       reaches the farthest bank.
It is sunset, and I am coming with you,
       my master.
From the high shore of the lake
       I turn back again to look;
On the green of the mountains
       white clouds are gathering.

P'EI: *Wide in the emptiness*
       spreads the water of the lake:
Its pellucid splendour
       reflects the hue of the sky.
I moor the boat to the bank,
       and whistle contentedly.
The freshness of the breeze
       reaches me from every side.

THE WILLOW WAVES

WANG: Divided into rows
      the slender trees go one behind the other:
Upside down, their image
      is interwoven with the limpid waves.
It is not like this
      beside the palace moat:
In spring the wind
      spreads the pain of farewell.

P'EI: *The willows*
      and their reflection
      unite into a single radiance;
Every breath of wind
      divides them
      with strands of silk.
You have found a good place
      in which to weave your shade.
No need then to be grateful to the hour
      that belonged to Master T'ao.

THE STREAM AT THE HOUSE
OF THE LUANS

WANG: Gusts of wind
     in the autumn rain;
The water falls headlong,
     it spills from the rocks in torrents.
The waves leap capriciously
     one on the other in flight;
The startled white heron
     comes down to earth again.

P'EI: *The voice of the stream*
     resounds to the farthest bay.
I walk along the shore
     towards the southern ford.
Here and there on the water
     ducks and egrets glide,
Always they return, impelled
     to the proximity of men.

THE SPRING WITH THE GOLD DUST

WANG: If every day I were to drink
        at the spring with the gold dust,
    I should live at least a thousand years
        and more.
    In the sky-blue chariot of the gods,
        drawn through the air
        by the multi-coloured dragon,
    With plumage and a staff,
        I should go in festal attire
        before the throne
        of the Jade Emperor.

P'EI: *It gathers together and overflows,*
        it glows and does not flow on:
    Gold and jade
        I almost seem to grasp.
    I salute the day,
        and my mouth is fresh
        with pure lymph,
    While I go alone
        to reach the water
        of the morning.

THE RAPIDS OF THE WHITE ROCKS

WANG: Limpid and shallow
        are the rapids of the torrent;
The green reeds
        I can almost touch.
The people from the huts
        to the east and west of the water,
Are washing silk
        by the light of the moon.

P'EI: *On tiptoe over the rocks*
        I return to the water's edge,
Playing with the water
        I feel a boundless emotion.
When the sun goes down,
        the cold settles on the river,
And the drifting clouds
        grow pale and evanescent.

PEI-CHAI

WANG: Pei-chai stands by the lake,
        to the north of the water.
  Among the various trees
        gleams the red balcony.
  Towards the south
        the wake of the river
        shows itself and withdraws;
  Gleams and is extinguished
        in the dark stretch of woodland.

P'EI: *In the mountains of the south*
        at the foot of Pei-chai,
  My hut looks out upon Lake I.
        every time I go
  To collect branches,
        in my cockle-shell boat
  I pass darnel and reeds.

THE HERMITAGE OF THE BAMBOOS

WANG: In solitude
     sitting in the hidden forest
     of the bamboos,
To the sound of the lute
     I whistle suspended notes.
In the secrecy of the wood
     I see no one:
The bright moon reaches me
     with its light.

P'EI: *I come and go*
     in the hut
     isolated among the bamboos,
Every day
     more familiar with the Tao.
I go and come back:
     there are none here
     but the birds of the mountain.
Where solitude is deepest,
     the people of the world
     cease.

THE BANK OF THE MAGNOLIAS

WANG: The tops of the hibiscus trees
           are in flower,
On the mountains
           the vermilion petals blaze.
Silent is the hut beside the torrent:
           there is no one at home.
By thousands and thousands the flowers
           open and fall.

P'EI: *On the green bank in springtime,*
           when the grass is thick,
The princely descendants
           are already glad to stay.
How much the more, if all around
           the bright-coloured flowering
           magnolias mingle
           with the hibiscus.

THE CASHEW-TREE ORCHARD

WANG: The ancient one was not
       a proud official;
He considered himself incapable
       of conducting worldly affairs.
Just as it chanced
       he took a modest office,
Inactive
       like these trees.

P'EI: *Love of idleness*
       soon became natural to me;
You see, here I am,
       faithful to the ancient promise.
Let us spend this day
       strolling through the park
       of the cashew-trees,
And let us renew together
       the joys of old Chuang Tzŭ.

THE GARDEN OF THE PEPPER PLANTS

WANG: A cup of cassia
        salutes the noble clan,
The mallow flowers
        I give to the sweet friend.
I offer pepper essence
        at the princely banquet:
O that you would descend,
        spirit of the clouds!

P'EI: *Red thorns*
        catch our clothes,
The scent of trampled plants
        follows our passage.
Fortunately they are useful
        for the cooking tripod:
May you be able, my master,
        to bend down and choose
        the perfumed seeds.

李長吉歌詩

LI HO
[791 – 817]

Backyard
Horses
Lamentation of a Bronze Camel
The Bronze Bird Platform
Lyre – A Korean Folk Tale
Li P'ing's Lyre Recital
Thinking
Ancient Arrow-Head
Magic String

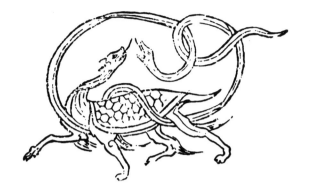

The Great Rebellion led by An Lu-shan and Shih Ssǔ-ming had been suppressed some thirty years earlier. The restored but not recovered empire of the T'ang was rent by political strife. Party alignments became clearer and the conflicts grew fiercer. Such was the dominant trend of events within the Imperial Capital. And outside it, the realm was divided and ruled by local commanders. The indications were that the dynasty was slowly drawing to its end.

In the world of letters, Li Po [701–762] and Tu Fu [713–770], the doyens of verse, were dead.

To the west of Ch'ang-an, in the year 791, Li Ho was born to a minor official, Li Chin-su – a descendant of Prince Chêng. The father's name was to be of immense importance to the new-born son. For when he was old enough for the *Chin-shih* nomination, people argued that he should observe the family taboo by refusing to sit for the examination. The father's name being *Chin-su*, the son ought not to be a candidate for *Chin-shih*. Han Yü, an eminent man of letters and a close friend of Li Ho, spoke in his favour, but to no avail.

Therefore the hope of his having a career as an official was dashed. The incident shows that the noble blood in his veins no longer afforded any prerogative and his resulting frustration may account for his eccentricity and cynicism.

Li Ho was thin, with joined eyebrows and long finger-nails. At the age of seven, his prodigious ballads and sonnets were a sensation in the capital. His method of composing poems contributed substantially to his reputation as an original. He used to go out riding on a donkey, taking with him his page boy who

[81]

carried a tattered bag on his back. Now and then he would stop, jot down a few words on a scrap of paper and tuck it into the bag. On returning home, he would sit down and expand the jottings into poems.

Among the most outstanding poets of the T'ang, Li Po was known as the immortal, Tu Fu the saint and Li Ho the ghost.

Li Ho died at the age of twenty-six.

BACKYARD

[1]
Flowers and weeds bloom before my eyes:
White and pink like a girl's cheeks.
To think that, during the night, they will wither;
Why not marry them to the east wind,
      without bothering a match-maker?

[2]
Not yet thirty, but well over twenty.
During the day, with only millet to eat,
      I am never free from hunger.
The old man who lives by the bridge
      pities me
And gives me a book on strategy.

HORSES

[1]
January roots are sweet;
And snow in the street
    looks like salt.
I am not sure of my own taste;
Be content with the bit.

[2]
This is no ordinary nag.
Once a star always a star.[1]
Let us knock on its old bones.
They sound like copper.

[1] Fang-hsü – the Horse – is one of the twenty-eight constellations

LAMENTATION OF THE BRONZE CAMEL

One April I had nothing to do;
So I went to one of the hovels in the east,
    to look for "flowers".
"Has someone written
    a farewell song to the spring?
Or is the bronze camel on the bank of the Lo
    weeping again?"
South of the bridge,
    horse-dealers were taking up their lodging;
And to the north of it,
    the ridge held many ancient graves.
The dealers went on drinking;
The camel all the while eternally weeping.
"Do not worry so,
Life is just like a candle."
"Perhaps the camel is tired of the sight
    of the giggling 'flowers',
So it is weeping in the night."

THE BRONZE BIRD PLATFORM

A lovely young girl brings up a jar of wine.
The autumnal scene extends over a thousand miles.
The stone horse lies in the early mist —
How can I describe the sadness?
The singing is now faint,
Because a wind comes up out of the trees.
Her skirt, long and heavy, is pressed against the floor,
And her tearful eyes are fixed on the flowers on the
    table.

LYRE – A KOREAN FOLK TALE

Early one morning, a Korean ferry-keeper saw a crazy old man
with a kettle in his hand trying to wade across the river. His
wife, chasing after him, shouted to him to stop. When the old
man vanished in the torrential water, she mourned him with a
song, accompanied on the lyre.

Master, master, where are you going with that kettle?
It is silly to follow the ancient example,[1]
         to jump in the river.

Master, master, there is a soft mat on your couch,
        and fish in your dish.
To the north of you, your worthy brother lives;
To the east of you, your niece.
Think of the gourds and the waving grain in your fields
And the sweet wine in your jars.
The wine needs drinking
        and the grain needs eating.

Master, master, will you not come back?
What can you achieve by drowning yourself,
Except to plunge your brother and niece in mourning?

---

[1] Ch'ü Yüan, an official and poet of the ancient state of Ch'ü went mad
and drowned himself.

LI P'ING'S LYRE RECITAL

The strings from the east and the wood from the west
    make the tall autumn loftier,
On empty mountains
    clouds stand still and crystallize,
Women's tears fall on bamboos
    and girls sigh,
When Li P'ing plays his lyre
    in this empire.

The jades of Koulkun crack to dust
    and the startled phoenix shrieks;
Hibiscuses weep pearls of dew
    and orchids smile;
In front of the twelve gates
    the cold light melts;
And the Heavenly King is moved
    by his twenty-three strings.

Thunder and storm rush out
    from a crack in the sky.
Then quietly comes the dream
    of an aged woman on an ancient mountain:
    she too plays the instrument,
To make old fish leap on waves
    and slender pythons writhe.
The last listener is left there,
    leaning against a cassia
When mist moistens the moonlight.

G

THINKING

Last year's song of farewell on the field-path
        still lingers;
Now you are far in the west,
        as your letter says.
Outside the window, flowers tremble
        in the April wind;
And my tears go to make the spots
        on a thousand bamboos.
My heart and the strings of the lute
Will tonight break and be joined together again.
Think of your white horse; think of your painted bow;
Think of the spring wind blowing everywhere.
Your heart is not made of stone;
And my beauty will not last for ever.
High up in the sky, the Milky Way hangs,
        for the remainder of the night,
But the ripples of stars are in vain,
        for there is neither bridge nor ferry boat.
The west wind is not here yet;
        my dragon shuttle grieves
To see my brows wrinkled while it weaves.
To my tearful eyes,
        the rivers and hills have no ending;
        the candle is forever blinking.
Since I have shut myself in this solitary chamber,
        how many times has the cassia bloomed
        and how many times the moon waned?
At dawn, a jackdaw in the wood caws;
The wind sweeps over the pond
        tinkling like ornaments of jade.

The sobering day puts an end to my dreams.
I can only go to the south of the bridge and listen
　　　to what the fortune-teller has to say.

ANCIENT ARROW-HEAD

Lacquer flakes, bone-dust and water
   made this vermilion colour;
And fearful, ancient stains
   bloomed on this bronze arrow-head.
Its white feathers and gold rings
   have now gone with the rain,
Leaving only this angular wolf's tooth.

Riding the plain with a pair of horses,
I found it, east of the courier station,
   among the weeds.
The long wind shortened the day,
   while a few stars shivered,
And damp clouds like black banners
   were hoisted in the night.

Thin devils and ghosts sang
   to the left and right.
I offered them pressed mutton and cream,
And crickets were silent, wild geese sick and reeds
   turned red.
The spirit of the whirlwind spat emerald fire
   to bid me farewell.

I stowed it away with my tears.
Its point, crimson and crooked,
   once bit into flesh.
In various districts, young riders exhorted
That I should sell it to buy firewood.

[92]

MAGIC STRING

[1]
The sun sets behind the mountains in the west
      and in the east the hills become dim;
A whirlwind smites the horses
      who seem to gallop on clouds.
The painted strings and unadorned flute
      play slow and quick notes
And the embroidered skirts rustle on autumn dust.
The wind brushes against cassia leaves,
      shakes down the seeds,
While vixens weep blood over the death of foxes.
The painted dragon with a golden tail,
      on that ancient wall,
Has gone to carry the imps of rain
      to the October pond;
The hundred-year-old vulture
      has turned into a wood elf.
When it laughs,
      green sparks shoot from its nest.

[2]
When the witch spreads her wine,
        clouds gather in the sky;
In the jade stove,
        fragrant coal burns.
Sea-gods and mountain spirits
        all come to take up their seats.
Paper coins crackle, turn into ashes,
        and dance in the whirlwind.
She plucks the lute made of love-sickness wood
        and adorned with a golden phoenix.
She mutters and beats the time
        by screwing up her eyebrows:
Come, Stars and Ghosts, and enjoy the feast.
When spectres eat,
        man shivers.
The sun sinks below the Chungnan Mountains
And the spirits become visible yet invisible.
Only her face reflects
        their anger or their pleasure.
Then a myriad chariots make ready
        for their departure.

李後主詞

LI YÜ
[937 – 978]

With the passing of the T'ang dynasty [906], the north-west of China ceased to play a leading role in Chinese history. Ch'ang-an has never since regained its glory. The commercial and industrial cities moved thence to the central plain, the south-west and particularly the Yang-tzŭ delta, where the émigré nobles, rich, skilled and educated, gave the country a new lease of economic and intellectual life, so that agricultural and industrial development coincided with the refinement of literary and artistic taste.

From the fall of the T'ang [906] to the establishment of the Sung [960], China was divided into many small states, of which one enjoyed hegemony. The hegemony passed successively into the hands of five different states; hence this period of fifty-four years came to be called the Five Dynasties.

The Southern T'ang was one of the states of that period, fairly large but not a hegemon. Its territory included present-day Kiangsu, Kiangsi, Anhwei and parts of Fukien and the south bank of the Huai River. In its short history of thirty-eight years [937–975], there were three kings and Li Yü was the last of them.

Li Yü, or Li Hou-chu, was born in the same year as his grandfather founded the kingdom and he succeeded his father to the throne in 961, a year after the establishment of the Sung, with the Sung Emperor as his suzerain. As a ruler, he lacked both political astuteness and military sagacity. The fate of his kingdom was doomed from the day of his accession. His naivety in administration may have been due to the fact that he was his father's sixth son and the throne became his only after the death of all his elder brothers. He was ill-prepared for his duties.

[101]

Nonetheless, Li Yü was gifted, sensitive and well read. Poetry apart, he excelled in calligraphy, painting, and music. He was also a great connoisseur of antiques and an ardent Buddhist. His handwriting is still to be seen on a famous painting of the T'ang dynasty[1] which was once in his collection and is now in that of Sir Percival David.

His life after his enthronement may be divided into two periods. In the first [961–975], he reigned over his state with his beautiful and talented Queen, O-haung, whom he married in 954. The Queen died in 964. Before that, he had been having an affair with her younger sister, whom he made his second Queen in 967. The affair was carried on in great secrecy as described in his poem, *A Meeting*.

Meanwhile the Emperor of Sung continued to put into practice the plan of unifying China. During his reign, Li Yü saw no less than three kingdoms destroyed by the Sung. The much-feared attack on his own kingdom was launched in 975 and within a few months, his capital, Chin-ling [Nanking], fell. He tried to secure the help of the Khitan, but failed. He also tried to commit suicide, but again failed. Therefore he dressed himself in white and surrendered.

Early in 976, he was escorted to the Sung capital, Pien-ching [K'aifêng]. Thus began the second period. He was made a Marquis and a General – both ranks being titular only – and lived in internment for almost three years. The short poems written during this period were as melodious as before, but painfully nostalgic and melancholy.

[1]A painting by Han Kan of a white horse – Chao-yeh Pai

On the seventh day of the seventh month of the year 978, on his forty-first birthday, he was commanded to take poison and died at day-break on the following day.

A MEETING

A thin mist veils the moon and the flowers.
Now is a good time to meet you.
My stockinged feet walk on the steps.
I carry my embroidered slippers in my hand.
To the south of the painted hall,
I tremble a short while in your arms.
"It is not easy for me to come out.
Will you make the best of it?"

H

ANGLER

Foamy tides, like snow-drifts, lingering;
A battalion of plum trees silently blooming;
A bottle of wine
And a fishing line;
Who in this world is my equal?

The oar rips apart the spring water
On which the leaf-like boat is floating.
A tiny hook dangles
At the end of a silk cord.
The islet is covered with blossoms
And my jug is full of wine.
Upon these thousand acres of waves there is freedom.

GARDEN

The garden, deep and serene;
The hall, vacant and small.
Now and then,
       washerwomen's pounding
       mingles with the wind.
In this eternal night,
       only a sleepless man hears
       the intermittent noises
Stealthily brought to the curtains
       by the moonlight.

NEW YEAR

Wind returns to this small court
      as lichens turn green.
Her eyes and the willow leaves
      make a sequence in spring.
Leaning against the balustrade
      she remains long in silence.
The new moon and the crackers
      are tediously the same as in the past.

The feast and the music have not yet ceased.
In the pond, ice is beginning to melt.
In the bright candlelight and the faint scent,
      and deeply hidden in this painted room,
My temples, overladen with thoughts,
      are white like frost.

DRINKING

Last night, the wind and rain –
Those autumnal sounds
    struck against the curtains and screens.
The candle wept,
    the clepsydra dripped
      and I leaned against the head-rest.
I rose, but found no peace.

All mundane affairs
    should be thrown into the river.
Life is just a nightmare.
The only safe path is down into the cellar.
Any other route is not worth the fare.

LOVE-SICKNESS

Her hair: tied up with a ribbon
And fixed with a jade pin;
Her flowing robes,
      soft and thin;
Between her adorned brows
      a shallow furrow.

October: too much wind
Accompanied by rain
Beating on two or three
      palm trees.
A helpless man
      in an endless night.

IN PRISON

A rule of forty years;
A kingdom of a thousand miles;
The princely pavilions that rose to lofty heights;
And the jade trees and bushes
      intertwined in a misty net —
All these had never known the clash of arms.

Now, captured and enslaved,
My limbs grow frail and my temples grey.
I shall never forget the hurried departure
      from the ancestral altar
When the court musicians were playing a song of
      farewell
And my eyes, imbued with tears, gazed at my maids.

HOW MUCH REGRET?

How much regret,
In a dream last night?
I wandered back to my hunting lodge,
      as in the past:
The chariots ran on like a stream
And the horses galloped like flying dragons.
The blossoms, the moonlight and the gentle wind
      were the joy of spring.

How many tears
On my face and cheeks?
I should not tell the secret in my heart,
Nor should you play the phoenix flute
      while our eyes are still wet.
For that would be too much to endure.

REMINISCENCE

The red of the spring orchard has faded.
Far too soon!
The blame is often laid
        on the chilling rain at dawn
        and the wind at dusk.

The rouged tears
That intoxicate and hold in thrall –
When will they fall again?
As a river drifts towards the east
So painful life passes to its bitter end.

THE PAST

The beauty of the scenery cannot sweeten
                         my bitter memories.
In the courtyard, moss spreads over the steps
                         despite the autumn wind.
My bead curtains hang down for days,
Since no one comes.

The golden sword has long been buried
And my ambitions have withered like weeds.
In the cool and still sky
                         the moon opens like a flower.
The shadows of my old palaces
Must now be aimlessly falling across the moats.

BIRTHDAY

Spring flowers and autumn leaves,
    will they never end?
How many things have happened?
In this little tower, last night,
    the east wind blew once more.
Can I bear to look back at the old country
    in the bright moon?

The carved hand-rails and marble steps
    must still be there,
But not my youthful cheeks.
How much sadness can I bear?
As much as an eastward-flowing river filled with
    spring water.

LIFE

The sorrow in your heart
      is betrayed by a few grey hairs.
Life is like empty mountain ranges
Where snow awaits your visits;
Yet you make your solitary retreat
      by the path in the wilderness.

SPRING SHOWER

Outside the curtains the rain is pattering
As the season draws to its end.
My satin bed-cover cannot keep out
      the chill at dawn.
In the dream, I forgot
      that I was in exile,
And for a time there was joy.

Never lean against the balustrade in solitude.
O, my mountains and rivers —
It was so easy to part,
But the return proves to be so hard.
Spring, will you go with the falling petals
      and the drifting currents
To paradise? Let me remain a while.

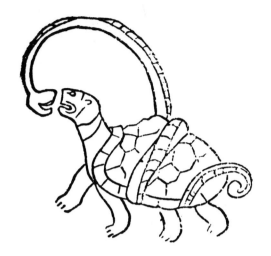

奉罕金厄之美沼臻瑨玉

匪之雕琴士綵芙蓉之羽性

九華備蜀之錦袋厨君裁

巡旦巴驪我低節心埽

吟東天柏梁銅雀上寧

下古時咏音携坂雜巨